5/4/2001

grades 3-4

To
DAN
and
JULIA

Printed on recycled paper

3 5 7 9 10 8 6 4 2

RUTH HELLER
WORLD OF LANGUAGE

MERRY-GO-ROUND

A Book About Nouns

Written and illustrated by
RUTH HELLER

The Putnam & Grosset Group

NOUNS
name
a person,
place or thing...

a **damsel**,
a **forest**,
a **dragon**,

a **king**.

These NOUNS
are all
COMMON,
and they're
very
nice,
but
PROPER
NOUNS
are
more
precise.
**King
Arthur**
is
this person.

This
place
is
Camelot.

PROPER
NOUNS
are
capitalized.

COMMON
NOUNS
are
not.

ABSTRACT
NOUNS
each
name
a
thought,
a
notion
or
emotion...

hope
and
love
and
chivalry,
courage
and
devotion,
justice,
truth
and
courtesy
and other NOUNS
we cannot see.

CONCRETE
NOUNS
can be
seen and touched,
tasted and smelled,
and heard...

persimmons
and **grapes**
and **onions**
and **pears**
and the
beautiful
song
of a
bird.

10

9

8

7

6

5

4

3

2

1

COMPOUND NOUNS
are
more
than
one
word...

countdown
is
joined
together.

Space Age
is separated...

and **merry-go-round**
is a NOUN that's
compound and…

it is hyphenated.

NOUNS are highly effective.

The last kind of NOUN is .

COLLECTIVE. A **tumble** of feathers, a **clamor**
of birds
and
a **riot**
of
colors
abound.

NOUNS are all around.

SINGULAR NOUNS are always one – PLURALS two or more.

Just add an **S** when there's more than one… That's the way it's usually done…

daffodils and **eyes** and **ears**, **beetles**, **bows** and **roses**, **ships** and **sails** and **cabbages**, **chrysanthemums** and **noses**.

But, it isn't
always
as easy as
that.

Here come some
exceptions.
Hang onto your
hat…

and other
headdresses.

Add **es** to NOUNS ending in **S**'s, **Z**'s and **ch**'s, **sh**'s and **X**'s...

albatrosses and **foxes**, **fezzes** and **boxes**, **radishes**, **squashes**, **macintoshes**, **galoshes**, **jackasses**, **eyeglasses**, **watches** and **witches**,

and more than one **ostrich** is always **ostriches**.

PLURALS
depend
on how the NOUNS end.
If
they end in a consonant
and then a **y**,
add **es** after
changing the **y**
to an **i**…
butterflies,
daisies,
pansies
and
berries,
blue-footed
boobies
and
yellow
canaries.

If a NOUN
ends in
f or **fe**
the **f** might be changed to a **v**.

Knives is the PLURAL of **knife** and **halves** is the PLURAL of **half**.

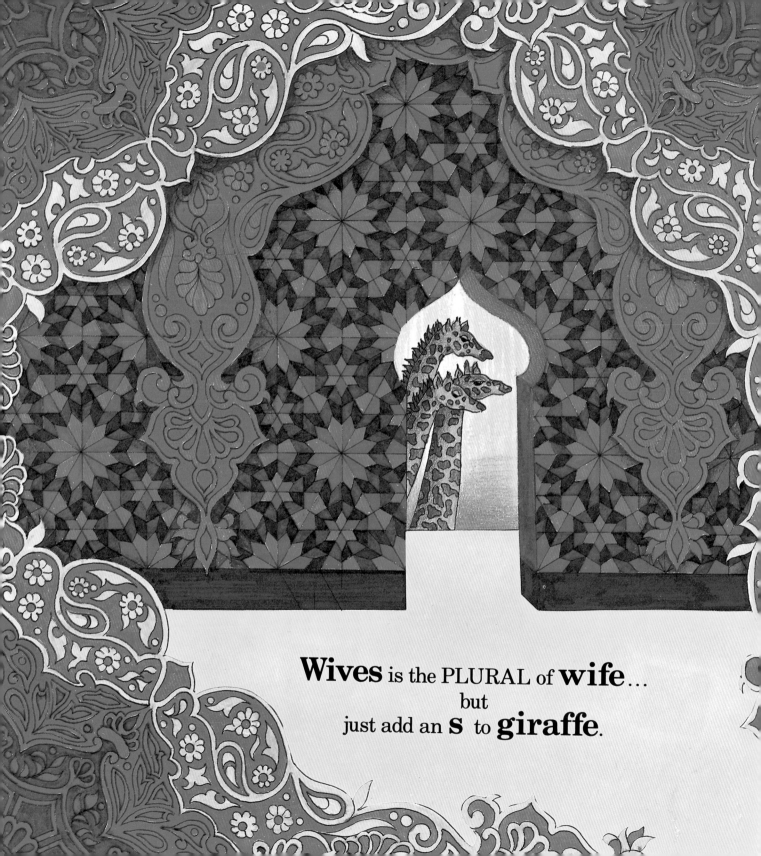

Wives is the PLURAL of **wife**…
but
just add an **s** to **giraffe**.

Which
way
should you go

when NOUNS end in **o?**

Add **es** to **tomato**
and also

potato
but…

s to **piano**
and as
to…

flamingo...
just add whichever
you wish.

The PLURAL of
fish
is **fishes** or
fish.

Some PLURALS remain
exactly the same.
Moose is
the
PLURAL of
moose.

Some
change in
the middle
like
foot
to
feet,

and
geese is the PLURAL of **goose**.

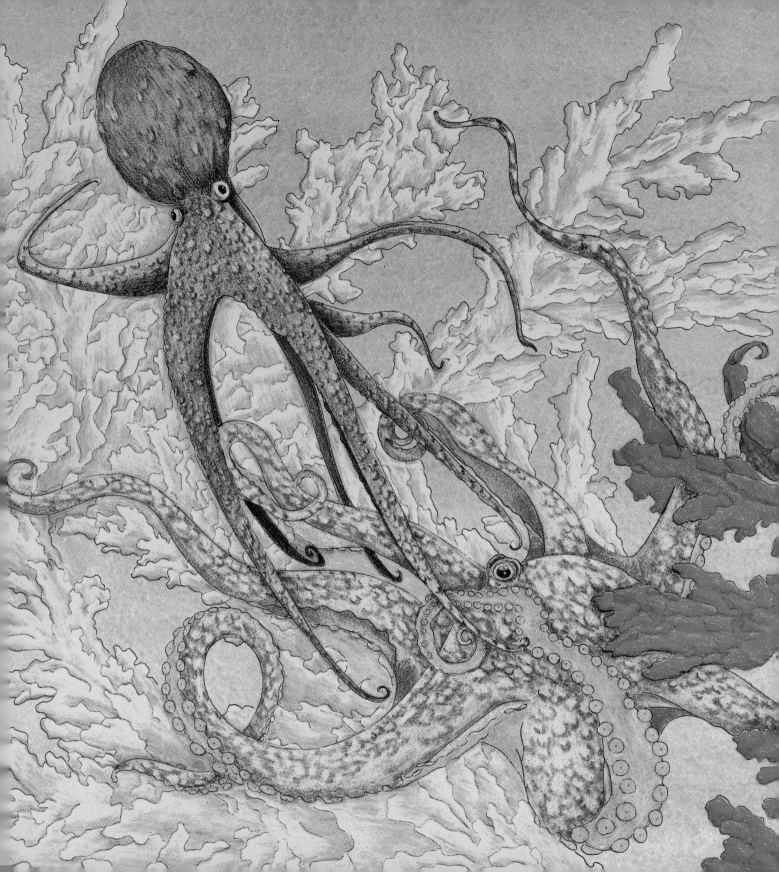

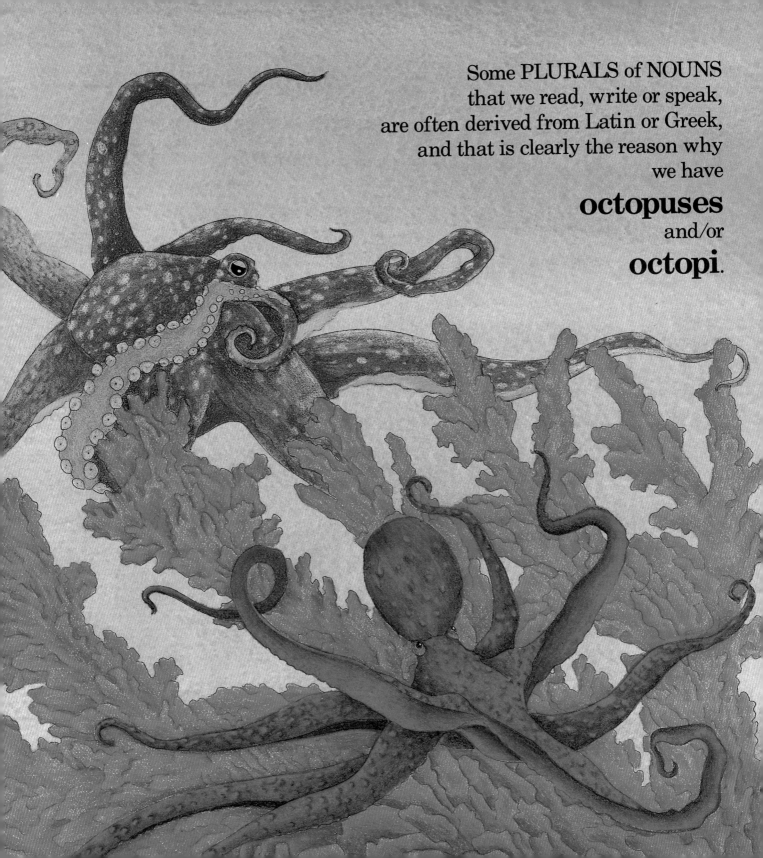

Some PLURALS of NOUNS
that we read, write or speak,
are often derived from Latin or Greek,
and that is clearly the reason why
we have

octopuses
and/or
octopi.

Now it isn't
really as hard as it
sounds, but be very careful of
PLURAL COMPOUNDS.

Trunksful
and
trunkfuls are equally fine…
but the **fleur de lys** is that small French design,
and you will find, as its number increases it becomes
fleurs de lys…and not **fleur de lyses**.

Add apostrophe **S**'s
when NOUNS are POSSESSIVE,
except…

when they're PLURALS
ending in **S**'s...

the **tiger's** stripes
the **lion's** mane
the **camels'**
obvious
disdain.

NOUNS
occur
soon after
a
DETERMINER.

DETERMINERS
are numbers…
26 **cucumbers**.

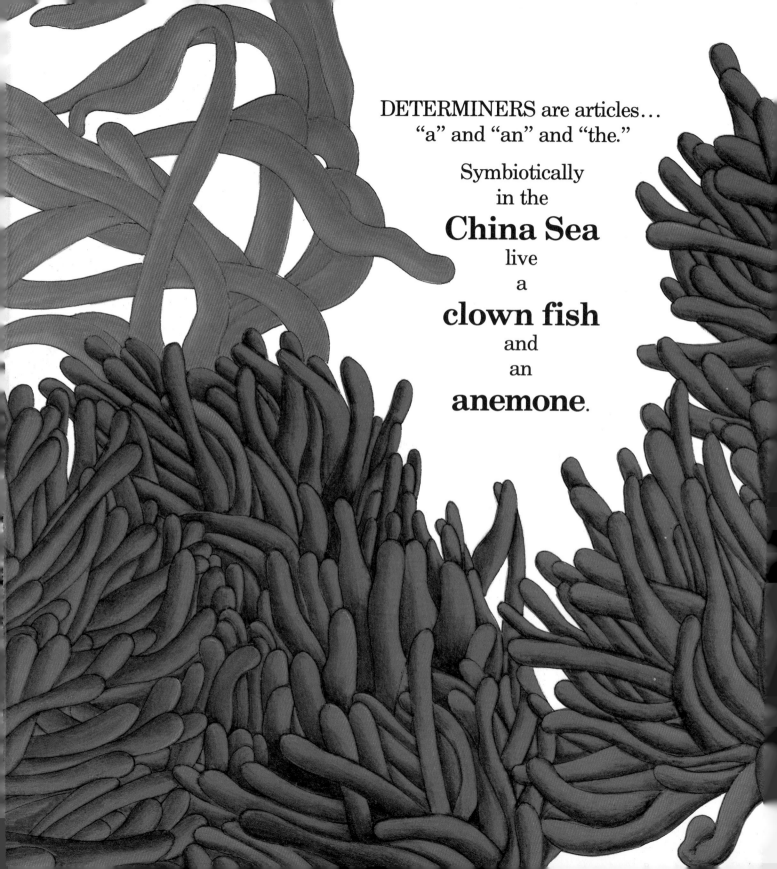

DETERMINERS are articles…
"a" and "an" and "the."

Symbiotically
in the
China Sea
live
a
clown fish
and
an
anemone.

A DETERMINER's a signal that a NOUN is on its way.

"This" is a DETERMINER....this **box**,

and so is "that"............that **fox**,

and "these" and "those"......these **hats**,

those **bows**,

and words that are indefinite...

some **daffodils**, a few **canaries**,

several **daisies**, many **berries**.

POSSESSIVES are DETERMINERS...

her **ship**, its **sail**, our **king**, his **reign**,

the tiger's **stripes**, the lion's **mane**.

DETERMINERS appear whenever NOUNS are near.

.

One last important fact...
whether COMMON or PROPER,
CONCRETE or ABSTRACT
or maybe
COMPOUND or COLLECTIVE,
each NOUN you will find
is more than one kind.

Whichever...they all are effective.